MAKE YOUR BUCKET LI A REALITY!

Find new life purpose, joy, and positivity through travel

Claire Maguire

Disclaimer

Contents

Preface

Traveling has always made a huge impact on me. My favorite childhood memories are of family trips from my home island of Jersey, Channel Islands, over to France. After just a short 35-minute boat ride, I found myself in an altogether different world! How could the food, the people, the language, and the customs be *so* different? I was fascinated. And hooked.

During my teenage and college years, every penny I earned went towards a trip. I jumped at the chance to guide British tourists and American High School groups in various places throughout Europe. It was a great opportunity... A chance to get paid to travel *and save up for more* travel?!

In 2017, after deciding corporate life wasn't for me (not enough vacation time!), I followed my heart and started my own travel business. It was a huge risk – but nothing had ever felt more right than signing my travel franchise papers. Indulging my passion for travel on a daily basis *and* sharing it with others – that's what I call living the dream! Everyone came to me for advice on planning vacations anyway, so I had no doubt this was the PERFECT business for me!

Flash forward to 2020 just as my business was gaining great momentum, Covid-19 hit. Lockdown. Borders closed. No travel. Hundreds of cancelled trips and clients.

As I sat in my living room, in isolation, I began to do a lot of thinking and self-reflection. I craved travel, but it was hopeless – impossible to go anywhere. Determined not to let it get me down (not to mention the kick my business was taking), I dreamed about the next trips I wanted to take and the amazing bucket list trips I wanted to offer my clients.

All my life, people had asked me how on earth I was able to take these exotic trips. With plenty of time on my hands, I decided it was finally time to share my secrets! I began to write an e-book. I put together an outline and spent a lot of time working on it. But then life started to return to 'normal'. As soon as travel was back on the cards, I was gone!

I spent most of late 2020 and all of 2021 taking advantage of every travel opportunity that came my way. Research trips, site inspections, the chance to learn more and build relationships with vendors. I was back to my norm of being busy and the e-book was cast into the bottom of my iCloud file barrel until further notice.

Ironically, when nearing the end of an idyllic trip with a client group to Tahiti in December 2021, I tested positive for Covid. Completely asymptomatic, yet continuing to test positive, I was unable to travel back home to the US for 14 days. I was 'stuck' in paradise!

Sitting on my balcony overlooking the ocean waves crashing below, I realized it was the perfect opportunity to turn the e-book outline into full chapters. Of course, it had to be the one time I traveled *without* my laptop, which meant laboriously writing every word on my iPad!

Now, many months later, the book has been completely reworked and edited into this new paperback version. I owe so much of the existence of this book to Trish Dickert-Nieves, Paul Stryer, and Anna Larras. I'll never be able to thank them enough for their advice, support, encouragement, and contributions.

The purpose of this book is to give you a blueprint to help you overcome your challenges, objections and doubts that hold you back from accomplishing your goals and making your dreams come true.

My wish is that by reading this book, you'll be truly inspired to do something life-changing for yourself and realize it's not *just* about the trip...

Claire 'UpintheairClaire' Maguire

Introduction

I've always been a go-getter. I was always chasing big dreams and seeking out new opportunities, even as a child. There were points in my life, however, where my energy was sapped and I lost my direction and drive. Something was missing...

Over the years, I hit rock bottom more than once. A broken marriage, loss of a career I loved, extreme financial stress, and heartbreak at a failed relationship I thought was 'the one'. It was hard to see a way out. I needed to find the motivation again - to move on with my life instead of wallowing and feeling defeated. When I look back, I realize that each time, I rediscovered my joy through travel. Taking off and exploring some place new, gave me fresh perspective and a different way to look at life. I didn't have a fortune in the bank. I just felt an overwhelming need to get away from it all, to give myself an opportunity to reset. So, I scraped together my last few dollars and made it happen.

It turns out, these trips weren't just escape vacations, they were an investment in myself. A much needed mental health reset that enabled me to rediscover my motivation, passion, and zest for life.

These days I'm a self-confessed 'Travelaholic'! I've explored 100+ countries and visited all 7 continents! In fact, travel has changed my life so much, that I've made it my business too. I've already helped hundreds of people take a trip they never imagined possible - a dream bucket list trip! You only need to look at my Facebook page to see that I'm officially living the dream. Not only because I get to travel often, but also because I get to change other peoples' lives through travel.

Can a trip *really* change your life? All the people I know who've overcome countless challenges to travel to their dream destination, would say YES without hesitation. They stopped wondering and instead experienced things they never thought possible. Felt feelings they'd never felt before. Learned something new and wonderful about themselves, something they're not prepared to give up. Many of them have already taken a second or third bucket list trip.

That's how I know that you can make your bucket list trip a reality and that when you do, you'll never look back.

Do you have an amazing bucket list trip you want to take? Somewhere you've been dreaming about since you heard about it, saw it on TV, or on the internet? What's stopping you?

- Does it feel too far-fetched, that there's no way you could make it happen?
- Too expensive?
- Can't get time off work?
- Worried about home obligations, or what your friends and family might say?
- You'd love to take a trip, but you've no idea where to start?
- A new adventure sounds great, but you're afraid of the unknown and can't possibly go it alone...

In this book, I'll share my proven framework for overcoming all the reasons why you think you should stay at home. I'll guide you step by step through an easy to follow process to plan and take your first bucket list trip. Together we'll explore those limiting beliefs holding you back and reframe them. Creating a new 'I can do this' mindset, whilst providing the practical tools you need to turn your daydream into real life!

I'm not kidding. [Insert your dream destination] here you come!

PART 1:

Is a Bucket List Trip for You?

CHAPTER 1:

Why Travel and What You'll Get Out of It

There are so many reasons why you should travel. I suspect you agree - it's why you're here, dreaming of your bucket list trip! My passport is packed with stamps, yet I continue to discover new whys. The benefits of travel really are never-ending.

Imagine laying on a hammock in the warm shade listening to the waves crash. You're on a tropical island with pristine white sand beaches and palm trees swaying gently in the wind. Smell the ocean and taste the salty air. You've not a care in the world. Right now, in this moment, everything is just... perfect.

Now close your eyes, take some deep breaths, and *really go there in your mind*.

What would you give to have this experience? What difference would it make in your life?

If a tropical beach paradise doesn't inspire you, there are countless options when it comes to travel. Our incredible planet is sure to host your dream destination. By the time you've finished reading this book, you'll not only have a bucket list trip in mind, you'll also be well on your way to making it a reality!

Before we move on, let's get really clear about **your personal whys** for wanting to travel. Understanding what's in it for you *and* the impact this is going to have on your life, is huge.

Grab a pen and a blank **notebook** that you'll dedicate to making your bucket list trip a reality! (If you don't have one, put it on the shopping list and use paper for now). Once you figure out your reasons, **write them down**. You're going to need them. They'll help you push through the doubts and fears that will attempt to hold you back. They'll remind you why you're going all out to make this thing happen.

EXPERIENCE DIFFERENT CULTURES AND WAYS OF LIFE

Have you watched documentaries about different people and places on TV? They're often fascinating because it's hard to imagine such a different way of life exists. When you leave the remote control at home and travel to a foreign place, the experience is tenfold. You're mentally stimulated in a completely new way. Everything you see feels fresh and different; you can't help but take it all in with a sense of wonderment and awe. Forget Sudoku – this is brainfood at its best!

When you travel, you feel alive. Are *you* ready to feel alive?

There's a huge and diverse world out there waiting to be explored. Every place has its own traditions, stories, unique history, nature, and architecture. Did you know that in Japan you should always walk on the left side of the pavement to avoid being swept away by the sea of people moving in the opposite direction? That in India, you should never point at sacred paintings or objects with your index finger, and only touch food with your right hand? And that the French never wait in line?!

Some countries have no electricity, plumbing, or internet. Kids don't have electronic toys or computers to pass the time; they use their imagination to create toys from whatever they can find. People live their everyday lives with perseverance and creativity.

When you travel, you don't just pick up a few interesting facts that might help in a pub quiz one day. You learn for yourself how people live, how they survive, and what makes them smile. And I can tell you, there's nothing more satisfying than a smile from a local – it's worth a thousand words and means you've made a connection. No TV show, book, or website can give you that.

It's in our nature to compare things, so it's a given that you'll compare any new culture with your own back home. But you won't stop at noticing the differences. You'll find fresh perspective and ask yourself questions about your own life - the kind of questions that will make it better and more meaningful. What might you do differently when you get home? Who or what could you appreciate more or feel grateful for? What if instead of getting frustrated at the usual things, you could stay calm and just do what needs to be done because it's not a big deal? This might sound far-fetched, but you'll be amazed at how humble travel can make you feel.

> **Travel opens your mind and helps you see the world through a new lens. When you apply that new lens to your own life, you'll see new possibilities you might never have considered.**

INDULGE YOUR CURIOSITY

Think about this for a moment... If you could open a door to **any** place in the world, where would you choose and what would you do?

Through travel, you get to pursue interests and passions at a whole new level.

What are you interested in? If you could pick any historical subject and be transported to the very place where history unfolded, where would you go? The Colosseum in Rome; the Acropolis in Athens; the Great Pyramids of Egypt?

What have you always wondered about? What it feels like to stand on top of the Great Wall of China? Or to snorkel with sea turtles on the Great Barrier Reef in Australia?

Have you always wanted to taste real gelato in Venice? To visit a local market in Provence, carrying a baguette under your arm? To crush grapes at a winery? Would you like to learn how to cook your favorite food from the locals themselves? See how perfume is made or chocolate is produced?

Are you a language lover? You've been taking night classes and would love the chance to practise your skills for real! Or maybe you're an arts and crafts enthusiast and need some fresh inspiration... Learn how to make Batik in Bali, coconut leaf hats and animal creatures in St Lucia, or cuckoo clocks in Switzerland!

Is nature your feel-good escape? Just when I think it's impossible to see something even more beautiful on our planet, a new destination surprises me. I recently visited Antarctica and it was one of the most serene, pristine, and exquisitely beautiful places I've seen. How about a safari or nature tour to see unique animals in their native habitats? I've been lucky enough to see some extraordinary sights including wild gorillas in the jungles of Uganda and Rwanda; orangutans in Borneo; the unbelievable parade of elephants crossing the Chobe River in Botswana; the annual migration of the wildebeest in Eastern Africa; and the 'Big Five' wild animals in Southern Africa! Which natural wonder are you dreaming about?

Whatever piques your curiosity, why not indulge it?

RELIEVE STRESS AND BOOST YOUR MENTAL HEALTH

Are you feeling stressed or stuck in a rut; empty and drained of energy at the end of each day? You're not alone. Studies suggest that most Americans are suffering from stress in one form or another. It's not surprising. With ever increasing demands placed on us at home and at work, it's easy to feel frustrated, overwhelmed, and anxious. Left unchecked, these feelings quickly escalate. I've been there – feeling so stuck I didn't even want to get out of bed in the mornings. I wanted to take action, get some perspective and 'think positive', but I couldn't find the get up and go to do it. That is until I went on a trip...

I'm no expert on stress. But through personal experience and having traveled with people who suffer from emotional or physical stress, I believe travel is an amazing tonic. It also sharpens your mind, stimulates your creativity, and helps you find new inspiration and direction.

Whether your itinerary is packed with sightseeing and activities, or you're planning to spend a few days in complete relaxation in a beautiful place, count on your stress levels dropping. Traveling takes you out of your daily routine and into new surroundings and experiences that reset your body and mind.

When you take a trip to a place you've wanted to visit for as long as you can remember and you intend to explore every nook and cranny, you won't have time to feel stressed. You'll be so distracted by new sights and experiences, that you'll forget about the things that usually wind you up! If on the other hand you allow yourself to take some much needed R and R, to relax in stunning surroundings and enjoy having someone else take care of you for a change, the stress will melt away. You've left all your worries behind and become present in the moment as you soak up your new environment.

Wherever you go, you'll discover a new culture. When you see people living with different values and priorities, your ideas change. This fresh thinking can help you consider the stress triggers in your life and realise that in the scheme of things, they're maybe *not that important* after all. And when you see people living in poor or challenging conditions, your own first world problems pale into insignificance.

If you've been through a big life change that's knocked you sideways, you might be experiencing heightened feelings of insecurity, self-doubt, or a lack of self-worth. A relationship break-up, job loss, empty nest, or the loss of a loved one can send you reeling. Leaving you feeling lonely and lost, with a lack of direction and focus. What if I told you that travel will help you conquer the deep depression you may be feeling? Taking a break from your daily life, will help you snap out of that dark place, and when you get home, planning your next trip will keep your mind occupied!

When's the last time you cut loose? Has it been a while? What stops you from being the person you are deep down? Judgement from others? Have you become an overly serious version of yourself in order to get by and live up to others' expectations of you? When you travel, you're incognito. You can be and do whatever feels true for you, without fear of judgement. Now, I'm not suggesting you do a Shirley Valentine – although it might be exactly what you need! What I am suggesting is that you give yourself permission to relax and go with the flow. To let your hair down and laugh. To try something new. When you travel, experience how it feels to let go, and feel the stress slip away. And if you fall in love with 'traveling you', which is my bet, imagine how this experience will change your home life too. Travel helps you reconnect with your true self.

> Taking a trip will change everything. Because everything is influenced by your mindset, and travel will change the way you think and feel about life.

How often do you unplug? Take a tech break for more than a few hours? We're so glued to our screens, that it's easy to forget what real excitement feels like, not to mention new physical and emotional experiences. There's no comparison between staring at pretty pictures of exotic islands or amazing cities, to actually being there. Stimulating your senses in real time and real life!

Now, I get that it's hard to even contemplate a trip when you're feeling stressed, demotivated, or run down in general. I mean come on... how do you start planning a dream trip when you struggle to write a shopping list?

All you need to do is keep reading.

GET OUT OF YOUR COMFORT ZONE AND BECOME MORE ADAPTABLE

When's the last time you got out of your comfort zone? Can you even remember? We're creatures of habit, but that doesn't mean it's good for us.

When I think back, I never imagined in a million years that I would do half the things I've done. I would have been too scared, not thought myself capable, or just never imagined opportunities like that would show up in *my* life. It turns out I wasn't giving myself nearly enough credit.

> I just needed to push out of my comfort zone *once* and experience something new and amazing. I felt truly alive. Naturally I couldn't resist going back for more!

I'm not going to sugar-coat this. You need to put your big girl (or boy) pants on and take a leap. Do something that feels scary, or uncomfortable. Something out of character for you. Something that pushes you out of your comfort zone and into the unknown. Because that's where you'll find the stuff dreams are made of!

> What could you do right now to get out of your comfort zone? How about deciding wholeheartedly to make your bucket list trip a reality?

That would be a great first leap! Albeit theory at this stage. If you really make it happen and go on the trip you've always dreamed of – now that'd be something.

Let's say you do it. You're on the plane, heading to that place you've been drooling over on Instagram for months. Then it hits you. You're about to have a brand new experience. What if you can't understand the locals? What if you don't like the food? What if you miss the bus? What if you can't keep up with the walking tour you enthusiastically signed up for months ago? What have you let yourself in for?

Welcome to the club. Do you think all the super confident travelers you spot at the airport started out that way? Most of them didn't. They started out just like you. Scared of the unknown. That's all it is – the unknown. When you don't know what's going to happen it's completely natural to feel uncertain. It's also completely new and wonderful! If only you can push past the (self-imposed) barriers in your mind and just give it a go. I can't tell you how rewarding it will feel. This is the beginning of your transformation!

Each time you take a deep breath, tell yourself it's going to be ok, and do something you never imagined doing, it'll get easier. Not to mention the tremendous sense of accomplishment you'll feel! Your self-confidence will soar, and you'll discover that you really are capable of way more than you thought. In fact, you'll start to wonder why on earth you've held yourself back for all these years. What *were* you thinking?

This adaptable new you won't just be good for trips. You'll feel empowered in all other areas of your life.

I've seen so many people find the courage, against all odds, to push out of their comfort zone and try something new. No one ever said they wished they hadn't tried. They all discovered a desire to do and experience more.

INCREASING EMPATHY AND COMPASSION

Travel is a humbling and character building experience. If you travel, you're among the privileged minority on our planet. It won't take long for you to realise how lucky you are. Even if you do feel stuck in a rut at home, or there are things you'd like to change in your life, you probably do have the power to change them.

Whether you realise it or not, you make assumptions and apply stereotypes that color your view of the world (we all do). Traveling challenges these thought patterns by exposing us to different behaviors, values, and lifestyles.

> Travel opens your minds and challenges your set ways of doing and seeing things.

Travel fosters empathy by teaching you how to be less judgemental about differences. Your version of what's right and wrong no longer applies when you realise there are many ways to look at life and situations.

When's the last time you took a moment to consider what a stranger might be going through? Maybe a cashier was rude to you, or someone took your parking space. Did you feel angry, or did you stop to think about the kind of day they might be having? Travel brings out a new quality – it makes you wonder. You probably stopped wondering about things at home a long time ago. But in a new place, expect to be interested in everything, and to want to find out more. Especially about people and their unique and diverse ways of life. As you discover their stories, get ready to feel a warmth of human spirit. Encounters with others lead to a new understanding and appreciation for different beliefs and behaviors. As a result, our interactions become more compassionate and less judgemental.

My travels in Africa made me realize that although the people living in remote villages had so little in the way of material possessions, they were clearly happy. They had a passion and joy for life, singing, dancing, running, and laughing. Their lives depended on protecting themselves from the dangers of wild animals and even other hostile tribes. As such, the villagers came together as a community to take action and make decisions for the greater good of their society. Of critical importance were the daily reports of lions in the area around the village, which created a response effort to protect fellow tribespeople and their cattle (the calves even lived inside their huts with the family!). Their priority is to protect life itself. Survival is the overwhelming force behind everything, unlike in Western culture, which values wealth, money, and possessions. Information about the outside world isn't relevant and doesn't impact their day to day lives in the same way it does for us.

This experience deepened my understanding of a culture and reality I'd only ever seen in a National Geographic magazine or in a nature documentary. It helped me better understand the beauty of African tribal culture and to appreciate a lifestyle so different from my own.

THROW EXPECTATIONS OUT THE WINDOW

I'm still learning that expectations are limiting. Even worse – they can set you up to fail. When's the last time you made plans and you were so looking forward to something, that you were imagining exactly how it was going to be in your head? Only... things didn't go to *your* plan, so instead of enjoying yourself, you felt frustrated and disappointed.

When you expect something – it's easier to feel disappointed. But when you expect nothing, every experience can be amazing in its own unique way.

So, if you learn one lesson before you travel – this is it. Why? Because you can't possibly create realistic expectations of something you've never experienced. Instead, get comfortable with being uncomfortable and try embracing everything! I'm not asking you to dance around a maypole (you can if you want), but just imagine making the decision to accept everything that comes your way at face value and without judgement. What's the worst that could happen? You slip into a feeling of disappointment? What's the best that could happen? You have the most amazing trip – you wring every last ounce of goodness out of it. Who knows... you might even abandon the usual expectations you set for yourself at home and look at your life in a whole new way!

APPRECIATE THE THINGS YOU'VE ALWAYS TAKEN FOR GRANTED

If you put your mind to it, you can probably think of a bunch of things you take for granted. And there'll be things you won't think about at all because you've never imagined not having these things. Like rooms in your house, a flushing toilet, a bed to sleep on, hot water, safe drinking water, or even the fact that you can read and write...

If you're going to Monaco and staying in a luxury hotel, your experience might not be a great lesson in appreciating what you take for granted at home! But if your bucket list trip takes you on an adventure in a developing country, get ready to experience a much more basic way of life. A way of life that makes you feel grateful for all that you have.

When you trek in Nepal, you stay in very basic 'teahouse' accommodation with squat toilets and access to an outdoor cold tap, which of course you can't drink from. There's only one thing to do – go with the flow because resistance really is futile! But when you get back to your hotel in Kathmandu, you won't believe how good it feels to sit on a Western flushing toilet. And a simple hot shower can feel like the best you've ever taken! It's *that feeling* again... you're thrilled to be alive!

"The magic thing about home is that it feels good to leave, and it feels even better to come back." - Wendy Wunder

You'll only truly understand the meaning of these words when you get home. On the one hand, it seems you're back where you started - same setting, same people, same problems. Yet you're not the same! You're changed, full of fresh knowledge, inspiration, and ideas.

I was feeling bored having lived my whole life in the same place. I desperately needed to get out and experience a change of scene. I realise I was only focusing on the negative – not much to do around, always meeting the same people, nothing changes... Now when I come home from my travels, I'm grateful for all this, plus I'm more open and I see only the positive!

MAKE NEW FRIENDS, IMPROVE SOCIAL SKILLS, AND BECOME AN INTERESTING STORYTELLER!

A truly special benefit of traveling is meeting new, like-minded people, and forming friendships that can last for years. It's so refreshing to meet new people with different backgrounds, stories, and ideas. These friendships can add tremendous value to your life – whether you think you need new friends or not! Most of my close friends today are people I've met on my travels. We've stayed in touch because we have a lot in common – after all, we chose the same bucket list trip!

If you're the quiet type and feel nervous about meeting new people, small group travel is a great way to go. From day one, you're part of a like-minded group and you're all in the same boat. So, you'll quickly find someone you feel good talking with. It's a great confidence booster! When you're on a day trip or excursion, there'll be lots of other foreigners – all curious like you and wanting to learn and experience your bucket list destination. It's a great foundation on which to start a conversation.

When you travel independently, you'll likely have lots of opportunities to meet other foreigners, as well as locals. Smile and say hi! You might chat for two minutes; you might become lifelong friends.

You can also improve your social skills by communicating with the locals. It's fun and much more satisfying to ask questions directly. The natives will appreciate your interest and you'll get the real story, as opposed to the guidebook version. You might feel intimidated or scared to try at first, but as soon as you do – you'll receive a warm response! Smiling is a universal way to break the ice, and if you've learned the basics – hello, goodbye, please, thank you, in the local language – you'll be an instant hit! I've managed to have conversations with people despite their extremely basic English. If you're a charades champion – your skills could come in very handy!

Getting out of your usual social bubble (friends and family), not only improves your social skills, but can dramatically improve your life!

Improving the quality of your social life isn't limited to the people you meet when you travel abroad. When you get home, you'll have lots of exciting and interesting stories to share. Instead of boring gossip and small talk, you'll have far more entertaining and inspiring things to say – about your travels, how different you feel, and that you're already planning your next trip!

Most of the people around you would much sooner hear about the time you sang Irish songs in a Dublin pub, learnt Greek dancing in Santorini, hiked in the remote Arctic, or ate Belgian fries with mayonnaise (not ketchup!). Or how about the time you tried fried worms in South Africa? That'll be sure to get some laughs! Telling stories is a great way to keep your trip alive, to inspire others, and to keep your dinner parties interesting!

One of my favorite travel stories is about the time when I was invited into a Maasai cow-dung mud hut in Kenya by a Maasai warrior. The tiny, round home had a big open fire in the middle, burning strong and giving off incredible heat. Two small calves were mooing in a little separated section of the home, and flies were buzzing everywhere. I was ushered to the far side of the main room by an excited child, only to see a lady on the bare dirt floor in full-on labor! The family were so excited – they believed that the new-born child seeing a blue-eyed blonde lady (me) would be blessed – as if by a guardian angel! It was so humbling, and I didn't have time to feel overwhelmed by the cries of the lady as her baby appeared right before us! It was truly an amazing tear-jerking moment in my life that I will never forget!

Another favorite experience was being hosted at the home of a lovely lady in Victoria Falls, Zimbabwe and treated to a feast of homemade dishes. I even tried the giant mortar and pestle to experience crushing corn into flour to make the main staple starch dish. What a chore! They certainly have to work for their dinners!

Or the time in Iceland when we stayed in a remote guest house in the countryside, hoping to see the Northern Lights. I'd planned to be there when the moon was at its smallest, to make sure it was as dark as possible. The weather was cold and clear, so we were super excited to see the lights.... Alas, there was no solar activity that night despite the 'perfect' conditions, so we didn't get to see them. We did however enjoy a fantastic meal of local lamb seasoned and cooked by our host in a deep pit with volcanic rocks, buried and cooked for hours. Tender, juicy and absolutely delicious!

CREATE PRICELESS MEMORIES

Travel literally opens a door to a whole new world. Once that door is opened, you can't close it. And believe me, you won't want to! To have more new experiences in a few short days, than during months or even years at home, is really something. What's that worth to you? What impact would it have on your life? *Might it be life-changing?*

Seeing and doing things for the first time with friends and loved ones creates a unique bonding experience. Something special that you'll share forever. Your kids might not remember what they got for Christmas several years ago, but they'll never forget a family trip.

Sure, you can buy more stuff for your house, or keep ordering those Starbucks daily. But imagine going on a bucket list trip instead... You can't put a price tag on the memories you'll create.

"Twenty years from now you will be more disappointed by the things that you didn't do than by the ones you did do. So throw off the bowlines. Sail away from the safe harbor. Catch the trade winds in your sails. Explore. Dream. Discover." - Mark Twain

BECOME AN INSPIRING ROLE-MODEL

As soon as you start planning your trip, your friends and relatives will pay attention. They might not admit they're envious, but you'll see it in their faces when they ask you about your plans. The fact that you're making this thing happen – you're really going on a trip to a destination you've always dreamed of; it forces others to ask themselves – *is it something they can do too?*

They'll expect to hear all about your adventures once you're home and they'll certainly want to see photos. What they won't expect is this alternative version of you. You're the same, but somehow different. You've a spring in your step. A carefree way of dealing with an annoyance. You're quietly confident. You know something they don't.

> It's hard to describe how traveling changes you. You have to experience it to know.

"I'll have what she's having." - When Harry met Sally.

Say no more. If others are as courageous as you, they'll start making their bucket list trip a reality too.

CHAPTER 2:

Create Your 'Trip' Bucket List

Now you need a bucket list. If you already have one, why not add more destinations? Or check in and see if the idea of visiting these places still gives you goosebumps!

It's time to let your dreams run wild and see where they take you!

If you're thinking, *what's the point?* That even if you *do* make a list, you'll never *actually* make it to these places... Just humor me (and yourself). It costs nothing to dream, and I'm guessing you're reading this book because a tiny part of you dares to believe you can find a way. That you *really can* make your bucket list trip a reality. I'm betting you can, and I'll help you figure out how over the next few chapters of this book.

Your first trip bucket list!

Grab a pen and your **bucket list trip notebook!** You're aiming to note down at least five bucket list trip destinations. They could be places you've always wanted to see, or places where you can do the things you've always dreamed of. Like swimming with dolphins in Mexico, seeing a real Geisha in Japan, or even hiking to Everest Base Camp in Nepal!

If your pen is flying over the page, it's great that you're already dreaming of specific destinations. It'll make the next steps in this book even easier to follow!

But if you're drawing a blank, don't worry! Here are some questions to inspire you. Take a few moments to consider each one and note down any preference, destination, or activity that comes to mind. At this point, no idea is a bad idea! So **don't hold back for any reason**, just write everything down!

- **Where would you love to go to?** A place you dreamed of as a child, or a country you saw in a documentary last year? Use your imagination; where can you see yourself? On a tropical beach; on the edge of a volcano; shopping in Milan; at the Great Pyramids?

- **What kind of vacation do you need?** Are you seeking adventure? An action-packed trip like hiking in Patagonia or climbing Mount Kilimanjaro? Or do you need some serious R and R – a lazy tropical island holiday with great weather, food, and cocktails on tap?

- **What's your ideal weather?** If your winters at home are freezing, it might be nice to spend a week defrosting in a tropical destination! Likewise, if intense heat isn't your thing, which cooler destinations do you like the sound of? Skiing in the Pyrenees; a cruise in Antarctica?

- **What do you want to experience?** Places are one thing. Activities are another. Have you always wanted to go Northern Lights hunting? To see the 'Big Five' wild animals in Africa? To stay in a traditional yurt? To finally practise your new language skills for real? To try all the French food you can get your hands on?!

- **What are you interested in?** How can you indulge your curiosity? What do you like learning about? What are you passionate about? What place do you find intriguing? What natural wonder do you long to see?

- Thinking about past vacations, **what did you really enjoy?** Was there anything you didn't enjoy that you'd want to avoid?

- **Need some more inspiration?** Visit my website to explore upcoming and future bucket list trips. Discover my own personal bucket lists and many more travel ideas in chapter 10.

Now you're thinking about all the amazing places you'd love to visit – you might want to do a bit of internet research to join some dots and fine-tune your list. It might be that you've always loved the *idea* of a particular place, but you don't actually know anything about it. Have fun looking up your top ideas! Check the images to see how they make you feel. Can you imagine yourself there? Ask questions about the weather, attractions, culture, food – whatever feels important for you. You'll quickly decide if it's a place that must go on your list!

When you read your list and feel a surge of excitement run through your body, you've nailed your first bucket list! I've suggested making a start with five destinations, but your list can be as long as you want. And now you're in the zone, thinking about where you'd love to go and what you'd love to experience, you'll keep adding to it over time.

Finally, to make your **first bucket list trip** a reality, you need to pick your TOP destination! Choose the place on your list that you *most want* to visit. Or the place that you feel most comfortable with given it's your first bucket list trip! Highlight your choice – that's what we'll be focusing on throughout the rest of the book.

So, how does it feel to know you're officially planning a trip to [your dream destination]?!

CHAPTER 3:

Travel without the hassle

You're all fired up and ready to plan your dream trip. There's just one problem. Where do you start? Organizing a trip can feel daunting, especially if you've never traveled abroad before. How do you make sure you've thought of everything, and know enough about your destination to get the very best out of your trip?

It's easier than you might think. Two great options to consider are: joining a small group trip or asking a Travel Expert to create the perfect independent travel plan. Both options remove all the stress from travel planning, leaving you to focus on making your bucket list trip a reality!

JOIN A SMALL GROUP TRIP

If you've never traveled and you're nervous about... well everything, joining an escorted group vacation is just the thing for you! Imagine traveling stress-free. No language barriers to navigate, no need to worry about getting lost, or driving on the other side of the road...

Everything is taken care of from the moment you arrive in your destination country. All you'll need to do is go with the flow and enjoy your trip of a lifetime!

Your guide will discretely deal with any issues that may arise. After all, you're traveling in a foreign country, and things don't always go to plan! But *you* won't need to give these things a second thought.

When you visit a dream destination, it's natural to want to experience the very best on offer. Making your bucket list trip a reality is a seriously big deal. So, having an average vacation is not an option! You want to see the most beautiful sights, try the tastiest food, attend the most authentic cultural show, get away from the tourist traps and see the **real** way of life, be safe... It's a tall order if you're relying on a guidebook. But not if you join a group trip – well, not if you join one of **my** group trips! I personally visit and explore every destination before creating a vacation. I experience the amazing, the good, the bad, and sometimes the ugly – so you don't have to! By the time a group trip is live on my website, it's been tried and tested by an expert (me!) and offers the kind of experience you'll simply love.

Ok, let's deal with the elephant in the room. Does the idea of joining a group of strangers for several days put you off? You're not alone. But guess what? I can almost guarantee there'll be other people in the group who feel just like you. I make a point of getting to know people throughout the planning process. As a result, I'm able to make early introductions based on who I think will get along. This works great if you're taking that leap and traveling alone for the first time. All you need is one like-minded person in the group, and you're set!

If you're traveling with your partner, friends, or family, joining a group can make your vacation even better! It goes without saying that you're taking a trip together to share the experience and create incredible memories. But it's also kind of nice to get a break from each other and to enjoy a bit of new company. It can be really refreshing to chat with new people – to hear their stories and share yours. It's probably not often you get the chance at home...

You could even make a lifelong friend – I have, more than once. Sharing the experience of pushing out of your comfort zone is a great recipe for bonding. You already know that your travel companions have chosen to visit the same destination, following the same travel plan. Perhaps it's not a long shot to think you might have lots in common!

Oh, and just when you start thinking you might have to spend every waking moment with your group, think again! Whilst you'll all be following the same set plan, there's plenty of free time built in for you to relax and explore on your own terms. So, you really can have the best of both worlds!

Now, if an escorted group trip isn't exactly what you had in mind, but you still feel like you need help with the planning, I've got another option for you...

LEAVE THE PLANNING TO A TRAVEL EXPERT

If you prefer to travel independently but you still don't know where to start, or you just don't have time to research and plan, get a Travel Expert on the case!

Planning a dream trip can be great fun, especially if you're doing it with a friend or loved one. But it does take time, and you need to be sure to have everything covered. The real challenge you face is that you don't know what you don't know. You can only take information at face value, and with so many different articles and opinions online, how do you know who to trust?

A professional Travel Expert makes it their business to know. When I plan bucket list trips for my clients, I know what questions to ask to understand what's going to make their dream trip. I'm also able to make suggestions and recommendations – often things they'd have never thought of.

The more you travel, the more you figure out what you should have thought of in the first place! Having visited 100+ countries, you could say I've got it down to a fine art. Plus, I've connections across the globe and access to some of the best rates and experiences! So, if you're determined to make this trip the best it can be – you can count on me to help make your dream bucket list trip a reality!

Are you already feeling curious about the kind of bucket list trips you could join, or take independently? Now's a great time to **visit my website** and get inspired!

www.bucketlisttraveltrips.com

I personally lead many of our group trips and I regularly add new trips and ideas. So, keep checking back, or better still contact me directly to let me know what you have in mind! Just **complete the contact form** so we can connect - that way I can keep you updated on new trips and travel ideas too!

If you're on Facebook, **join our Groups** and be a part of our Bucket List Travel community.

www.facebook.com/groups/islandgirlbucketlisttrips
www.facebook.com/groups/bucketlisttraveltrips

PART 2:

How to Overcome Your Challenges

CHAPTER 4:

The Mental Challenges

Let me guess... as much as you'd like to, you couldn't possibly consider a trip like this.

Could you?

Believe me when I say you're not alone. If you've never traveled, the prospect can feel extremely daunting – impossible even. Like it's something available to other people, but not you.

It could be that you're at a low point in life having been through a recent change that's knocked you sideways. The idea of venturing into the unknown feels impossible right now.

Or maybe it's just too much like hard work.

Sure, the idea of taking a dream trip sounds great. But then you find yourself thinking of a dozen reasons why you shouldn't...

I've seen hundreds of people *just like you* overcome their own personal challenges and make it happen. That's how I know you can too. And if you do, it'll be one of the best things you've ever done.

Let's say for a moment that you don't make it happen. You don't overcome the challenges playing on your mind. You don't believe you can save enough money or get time off work. It all feels too hard, and scary. You're already feeling stressed and tired, why would you consider taking on something like this? Especially if you're not in a position to just book a trip and pack your suitcase when the time comes.

Instead, you truck along. Same old same old. You don't shake things up. In fact, you know exactly what to expect day in, day out. It's comfortable and safe. It's not exciting, but it's not scary either. You won't see that place you've always dreamed of or feel emotions you've never felt before. Maybe you'll regret your decision one day, but you'll worry about it then.

How does that make you feel?

We allow so many things to hold us back. We establish mental blocks like a self-protection mechanism, but what they actually do is stop us from living a full life. How often do you make an excuse to yourself, which gives you permission to give up on something that feels a bit hard? We all do it! Ask something of yourself that's outside your normal thought patterns or behaviors and watch what happens...

It's easier to decide in advance that you won't fail at accomplishing your dreams, by blaming others and external circumstances for not even trying.

Let's take a closer look at some of the objections that might be holding you back.

YOU'VE NO RIGHT!

What will people think when they find out you're planning an amazing vacation?

I hope that everyone will be thrilled for you – they should be! But jealousy and insecurities are likely to draw out at least one naysayer...

- Oh, you're *really* going to Italy? How will you manage *that* when you've never even been to the East Coast?
- What about all your responsibilities at home? Who's going to take care of things when you're away?

- What will everyone think, what will they say?! This is so out of character for you!
- Why do you want to take a trip anyway? You've got everything you need right here.
- That's nice dear. What time will dinner be ready?

You're intending to do something incredible; to have a once in a lifetime experience. Be prepared to discover that some people around you not only feel jealous that you're doing it, but also resentful that they didn't think of it first. The important thing to remember is that the issue lies with the other person. It's not about you at all, so there's no need to feel bad about their reaction. Instead, try to understand they're reacting this way because something's going on in their life that makes them unhappy. Stay positive and change the focus of the conversation. If they've got nothing nice or helpful to say about your trip, they're not the right person to be talking to about it. Instead, surround yourself with supportive people who believe in you. And by the way, this is good advice **all** the time, not just when you're making your bucket list trip a reality!

If you experience pushback from your nearest and dearest, find the right moment to sit down with them and explain **why** you want to take this trip and what it means to you. What might a great compromise look like? Is there something they've always dreamed of doing that you can help make a reality?

Are *you* having doubts?

Maybe you think you're not good enough? That you don't deserve to be happy or to have amazing things happen to you?

I'm here to tell you that **you can make your bucket list trip a reality**. But to do so, you need to be kind to yourself. Tell yourself often, that *you can and will find a way to take this trip that you know will change your life*. It might not be easy, but the best things in life rarely are. So, have patience and forgive yourself when something doesn't go to plan, or you start doubting yourself. Take a break and remind yourself why you're doing this. Then focus all your attention on the next thing you need to do to make your trip a reality, no matter how small. We'll explore this some more in chapter 9.

YOU'RE STUCK

If you're just plain stuck and can't see a way out, **this trip is it!**

Take it from someone who knows. Travel *is* your escape and will open the door to a whole new existence – a more fulfilling life. Sure, it's going to take some effort to make it happen. Effort that's hard to muster when you're in a slump. But that's why you're reading this book. You know you need to try something new and different; that if you don't switch things up, you'll live to regret it.

So, don't.

Grab your **bucket list trip notebook**, write out these statements, and fill in the blanks:

- I want to take a trip to _____ because _____.

Think about why you want to travel to your dream destination – what excites you about it?

- Taking this trip is really important to me because _____.

Write down all the reasons why this trip is important to you.

- If I don't take this trip _____.

How will you feel and how will it affect your life?

Now, each time you start feeling stuck or anxious, look back at your notes and remind yourself **why you are going to make this trip happen!**

YOU'RE SCARED

In chapter 1, we talked about getting out of your comfort zone. It's completely normal to feel scared, anxious, or nervous about something you've never done before. Taking this trip *is* a big deal. It's also the ticket to discovering a new version of yourself. Someone with the courage to try new things and start saying, *"yes, I'd love to give that a go!"*

So, what exactly are you afraid of? Can you pinpoint it? Sit quietly for a moment and really think about where that feeling of dread is coming from. Often, we're just scared of being scared. *Think about that for a moment.* It means you're scared by the idea of being scared, but you're not actually scared of anything real at all!

If you have identified a real fear, once you can see it for what it is, you can face it head on and determine what you need to do to overcome it. Try searching for ideas online or confiding in someone you trust.

Fear of failure is extremely common and something you could be experiencing. For now, I'll just say this: keep reading. I get that it may still feel impossible to make your bucket list trip a reality, but that's because we haven't got to the 'how' yet...

YOU'RE STRESSED AND TIRED

If you're already suffering from stress and exhaustion in your daily life, no wonder the thought of taking a trip wears you out!

But if you make it happen, you'll be giving yourself the chance to rest and reset – for real. And things will look and feel very different when you get home.

This trip will help you:

- take a real break from your tiring routine
- reset your mind and body
- snap out of a dark place if that's what you need
- discover new inspiration and direction
- cut loose and be yourself without fear of judgement
- consider the stress triggers in your life and figure out what's truly important
- learn how to look at and react to things in a different way – which could come in very handy once you get home!

What's that worth to you?

YOU'RE DISORGANIZED

It's hard enough to get ready for a weekend away just an hour up the road. So, the thought of organizing several days abroad is enough to send you reeling! How could you ever make it work?

Just because you're not the most organized person in the world, doesn't mean you can't make your bucket list trip a reality. All you need is a little help. The fact that you're reading this book and you've got this far, shows that you want to take this trip, and you're determined to find out how.

What you need is a plan, and to breakdown the seemingly mammoth task of organizing an overseas trip into lots of mini tasks. You need them to feel small enough to not be overwhelming, and easy enough that you can check them off your list without too much effort or stress.

By the time you've finished this book, you'll have a realistic and achievable step by step plan. And don't forget – you don't have to organize *everything*, because you can choose to join an escorted group or have a Travel Expert plan your dream trip for you!

So, have you written your 'trip bucket list' yet, or did you put it off until later…? If you haven't decided on a destination that sends a rush of excitement through you, head back to chapter 2 before you go any further. It's that specific dream and the desire to make it come true that will help you push through the necessary 'doing' bits!

YOU CAN'T AFFORD IT

We'll get to this in chapter 6!

CHAPTER 5:

You're all fired up having decided: **you're taking this dream vacation!**

Go you!

It's a done deal in your mind. But then the thought hits you. What about your job? What about the kids? Who'll feed your cats? There may be several things you need to work around or find a solution for... *Is that a feeling of self-doubt creeping in?* It's ok! You got this. Just remind yourself that you **can** do this and all the reasons **why** you want to.

Mini crisis averted? Good. Let's have a chat about logistics and figure out how you'll tackle each one.

TIME OFF WORK

Now you've got a destination in mind, you should have an idea about how much time off you'll need – a few days, a week, 10 days? (If you don't, you can revisit this chapter later).

If you need more days than your annual entitlement, or more than you're supposed to take at one time, you'll need a conversation with your boss. There are many options to consider and propose. If your boss is reasonable and you're a valued employee, you should be able to find a mutually agreeable solution.

Preparing for your meeting

Make sure you're prepared to explain clearly what you want to do and **why**. Remember, this is *way more* than an average vacation. This is about making your dream come true! Your boss will be more likely to say yes if he/she understands how important this is to you.

Be ready to talk about all the great things you've done for the company and the consistent effort you put in. What recent contributions or achievements can you mention? How about a reminder of your last great review?

Don't forget to explain that you'll return to work feeling properly rested and refreshed, which could be great for your productivity and motivation!

Before your meeting, it's also worth checking your company policy. You may discover some helpful information, or new options you weren't aware of.

Potential options you might explore with your boss

- **Ask for the time off way in advance** – explain that you want to give your boss plenty of time to organize how they'll manage without you. You may even share ideas about how your responsibilities can be covered. For example, your colleagues may agree to take on extra tasks whilst you're away; you can do the same for them another time.
- Request to set up some special provision to accumulate some **personal or compensation days**. Could you work some overtime and then take extra time off in lieu of pay?
- Is **unpaid leave** an option for those few extra days?
- Is it possible to **use sick days** as vacation days?
- Does your company have a short-term **sabbatical** opportunity that you might be entitled to?

If your boss is not reasonable...

Well, you never know until you try. So, give it a go and see what happens. If it really is a NO, and you've worn out your list of ideas, consider whether there's someone else in the company you might speak to. Perhaps HR or another manager? You might not want to rock the boat, but are you prepared to put your life on hold for a boss who doesn't respect you?

You may even decide it's time to consider leaving the job that's been holding you back and start looking for one with more benefits – increased income, more vacation time, greater flexibility... Because we're not just talking about you taking a trip here, we're talking about you living your life to the full and doing things that make you happy.

YOUR DEPENDENTS

The kids – if you're planning the honeymoon you never had chance to take, or you're desperate to spend some quality time alone, you'll need someone to take care of the kids. If you plan your trip well in advance, can you ask grandparents, siblings, or cousins to take care of them? Or even a close family friend you trust who might be prepared to help you out?

If you've exhausted all your options without any luck, maybe that 'adults only' trip needs to wait. But what if you could take a trip *with the kids* and stay in a family friendly resort with lots to keep them occupied? Think kids' clubs and even inhouse babysitters! That way, you don't have to put your dreams on hold. You'll spend quality time alone, plus you'll create amazing family memories that your kids will treasure for life!

Elderly relatives – are you on regular visiting duty for a nearby elderly relative? Who can you ask to pick up your visits, or at least stop in once or twice whilst you're away? A sibling? A friend of your relative?

Or would it be ok to explain that you'll be away for just a few days; that you've done the grocery shopping, etc. That you simply can't wait to tell them all about your trip and share photos once you get home! Can you ask a friend to be available on the phone in case of an emergency?

YOUR PETS

It's a given that you'll need to find a suitable care option for your pets when you're away. Here are some ideas to consider. As with your job and the kids, be sure to plan ahead!

- Leave your pet at home with access to plenty of food and water and ask someone (maybe a neighbor) to stop by, check on your fur baby, and top up their food/change their water, daily if possible. This can be a great solution for very independent cats or caged animals like rabbits, hamsters, mice, etc.

- The same as above when you don't have a neighbor or friend nearby that you can count on... Find a local business that specializes in taking care of pets and book someone to come to your house for a few minutes every day.

- Arrange for your pet to stay with someone you trust who'll take good care of them.

- Organize a reputable animal loving house sitter – not only will they look after your pets, but they'll take care of your house too! A great option when you have dogs who need regular walks *and* company. (Or a cat who doesn't like being left alone!).

- Book a kennel/boarding house for your dog or cat.

HEALTH CONCERNS

If you have any health concerns whatsoever, seek advice from your doctor or medical professional **before** you book your trip.

WHO'LL WATER THE PLANTS?

Easier to sort than the kids and the dog, but still a valid concern if you'll be away for more than a few days. Who can you ask to come by and water your plants, or lawn whilst you're away?

A quick search on the internet 'how to water plants while on vacation' will give you lots of ideas to stop your indoor plants drying out.

CHAPTER 6:

The Financial Challenges

Let's get into the most likely objection you have for taking this trip. **You can't afford it.**

I'm guessing you fit into one of two categories:

1. You have the money or can save it easily, but you can't justify spending it on a trip, or on yourself.
2. You don't have the money and can't imagine being able to save enough.

Let's unpick them both.

You have the money or can save it easily, but you can't justify spending it on a trip, or on yourself

It's a lot of money. Possibly more than you've ever spent on yourself at one time. How can you justify it? Especially when you'd have nothing concrete to show for it.

What if you think of it as an investment in yourself? It's not just about the few days you'll be away having the trip of a lifetime – it's going to help put a fresh new spin on your whole life!

There are so many reasons to travel and to give yourself permission to do this one amazing thing for yourself (chapter 1). Think about it... In the grand scheme of your life, you *can* afford this, and don't you owe it to yourself?

If your trip isn't everything you hope for, you'll know that travel isn't for you. But if it is... well, it's going to give you a sense of accomplishment and joy that will change everything!

Truth time

It's time to hold a mirror up and ask yourself:

- How much do you want this?
- How important is this trip?
- What's it worth to you?
- Do you deserve this?

At this point, you know what's at stake. So, what does your gut tell you? Is this something you can forget about simply because it's too expensive? Or can you find a way for it to be ok to do this incredible thing for yourself?

You don't have the money and can't imagine being able to save enough

Here's the thing. You *can* save enough money – I've seen many do it against all odds. It might take time; you might plan your dream trip 18 months or even two years out. You'll probably need to make some sacrifices or change spending behaviors along the way. But **you can** find a way to save enough money – *if you really want to.*

The first hurdle to get over is your mindset. I'll let you into a secret – when you say, "I can't afford it," you're reinforcing a belief pattern in your mind that creates your reality. Think about it like this: when you wake up in a good mood, you're more likely to have a good day and take any problems in your stride – right? But when you wake up in a bad mood, everything seems to go wrong, and you can't catch a break. Instead, you end up feeling even worse and grouchy, and you put it all down to 'having a bad day'. This is a simple example of how your mindset can affect your day, and of course your life.

So, when you say, "I can't afford it," **you'll be right** – whether you

can or can't. But the moment you say, "YES! I can make it happen –
somehow, I'll save the money!" You switch from focusing on *lack* – what
you don't have, to focusing on the idea of *abundance* – that there's
enough (resources, wealth, love, opportunities) to go around for
everyone.

The point is, when you decide for real that you're going to succeed
and focus your attention on making your bucket list trip a reality, your
whole mindset changes. Something you thought was impossible
suddenly **becomes possible**. With this positive mindset you'll find it
easier to overcome challenges and take clear and purposeful steps
towards making your dream come true.

"Where focus goes, energy flows." – Tony Robbins

> Try it. Tell yourself out loud, "I'm going to find a way to save enough
> money to take the trip I've always dreamed of." Now believe it. Know
> it. Have unwavering faith in your ability to do this.

Are you sitting a little taller? Can you feel the possibility in your
heart? Are you sensing the power you have over your own life if only you
choose to get in the driver's seat? This is just the beginning. You're
tapping into a whole new inner strength, which will resonate
throughout your life and your interactions. The more you focus on what
you want, the more important and real it will become.

Now, you've just got to decide how you'll put the money aside and
figure out a plan...

How much money do you need?

You need to have a reasonable idea about how much your trip will cost,
to know how much you need to save, and how long it's going to take.

If you've decided to take one of the bucket list trips on my website
you'll have an idea of cost – don't forget to add your international
flights (you can check prices on skyscanner.com) and any other
excluded expenses (extra nights, excursions, travel insurance, etc.).

Or, if you're planning to take an independent trip, I can help provide an idea of cost.

Once you've got a figure in mind, it's easy to work out your savings plan. For example, if your trip will cost $2,700 and you want to take the trip in 18 months' time, then you'll need to save $150 per month.

If you've no idea about the cost right now, you can work it out once you've firmed up the details of your trip in the next chapter, then come back to this section.

Ways to help you save some money every month

Do a realistic household budget and work out how much disposable income you have available to save each month. You might be surprised. It's easy to spend money when it's there, but if you transfer some into a savings account *before* you have chance to spend it, problem solved! See chapter 8 for help with calculating your budget.

What can you cut back on/do without for a while? Look at the 'non-essential' spending in your budget. Daily Starbucks? Can you make your lunch and take it to work instead of buying fast-food every day? What are you putting in your shopping cart that you don't really need? Can you skip the alcohol when you eat out?

Do you have any unused/unnecessary subscriptions? A gym membership that's going rusty or a subscription to a TV channel that you hardly watch. It's time to be ruthless and cancel any services you don't need!

How can you be thrifty? How much do you spend on cards and gifts? What could you make instead for a fraction of the price? It's the thought that counts, and homemade gifts are always well-received! Could you ask your talented friend to do your nails instead of going to the salon every month?

Do you have unwanted/unused/surplus items that you can sell? There's a huge market for second-hand goods. You just need to find the right platform to advertise on. Before you post your listings, have a good look around and see how other people describe their goods. Which would you be most likely to buy? This will help you write a compelling description and make the sale! Try OfferUp (offerup.com), eBay (ebay.com), or even Facebook (facebook.com). But be sure to check platform guidelines to protect yourself from potential fraudsters.

Ask for extra hours/overtime – if this is an option, it's a great way for you to earn some extra income that you can transfer straight into your savings account!

What can you do or create that other people want and would be prepared to pay for? Are you well known in the neighborhood for your delicious baking? Do you have a flare for mending and adjusting clothes? Could you wash cars, or do some ironing for a bit of extra income?

A side job/side hustle - could you break out the server apron or bartend for some extra tips? Get a retail job in the evenings or on weekends? Maybe you could use your skills and certifications to teach yoga or dance on the side? You might even discover that your side hustle becomes your passion and main income source – just like being a Travel Planner became mine!

Every little helps, and you'll soon be on your way to saving $150+ every month!

     Be sure to create a specific savings account for your BUCKET LIST FUND. And if possible, set up an automatic payment every month. Keep track of your fund and proudly watch it grow! It's an amazing feeling – the more you save, the closer you are to your goal and the more excited you'll feel! Maybe even throw in an extra $5 when you have a little bonus money or spend less on something else. I'm telling you, once you start saving for your dream, it's addictive!

So, what's holding YOU back?

We've covered lots of different challenges and objections, some of which probably apply to you. In chapter 8, you'll figure out how to deal with them one at a time. Plus, we'll walk through your finances and help you create a plan to save the money for your trip.

But first, don't you think it's time we put the spotlight back on your dream trip for a while?!

PART 3:

Make Your Bucket List Trip a Reality!

CHAPTER 7:

Design Your Bucket List Trip

Now for the fun part – firming up the details of your bucket list trip!

If you're feeling a little hung up on the challenges standing in your way, set them aside for now. Until this moment, your trip has been theoretical – little more than a wonderful idea you're dreaming about. In this chapter, you're going to make it concrete. Then *you will* feel ready to find creative solutions and give any lingering objections their marching orders!

In chapter 9, we'll dig into how you'll stay motivated to achieve your plan and reach the moment when you're packing your suitcase! But first, let's lock in where you want to go, when, and all the other exciting details!

You'll need your **bucket list trip notebook.** Work through the following steps and write down as much detail as you can.

> **The key to your success is being absolutely determined to make this trip happen and to feel overwhelmed with excitement by the idea of finally seeing your dream destination!**

You might complete this exercise over several days – that's ok! This is *your plan* for making your dream bucket list trip a reality. So, take your time; **enjoy the process and believe in your ability to make it real!** If you need some information about your dream destination, jump online and see what you can find.

1. **WHERE will you take your first bucket list trip?**

You wrote down your dream destination in chapters 2 and 4 – does the idea of visiting this place still make your hairs stand on end?! Now you feel more confident, is there a place you'd just LOVE to visit that you ruled out earlier because you thought it would never be possible? Now's the time to decide...

2. **WHY do you want to go there?**

*If you haven't already noted several compelling reasons WHY you've chosen this destination, now's the time. Having a very powerful WHY is the **key** to achieving your plan and taking this trip!*

3. **WHEN will you go? (Pick a target month and year)**

You'll want to allow plenty of time to save up, prepare your trip, and to visit your dream destination at the right time of year. So, before you decide WHEN to go, consider the following:

- *How much time do you think you'll need to organize logistics?*
- *Will you be celebrating a special occasion on a specific date? (Big birthday, Anniversary, Honeymoon, Graduation...)*
- *When will you have saved enough money for your trip?*
- *When is a good time to visit your dream destination? (Check the annual weather forecast, peak tourist times you may want to avoid, or when a particular phenomenon you'd love to see usually happens...)*

4. **WHO will you travel with?**

Are you traveling with your partner, family, or like-minded friends? You might choose to travel alone – it really is an amazing experience! Think about what you want to get out of this trip and therefore who you'd love to share it with, if anyone!

5. **WHAT kind of trip do you want to take?**

In chapter 3, I explained two great options to make your first trip much easier and less stressful. Choose to join an escorted small group trip or have a travel planner organize your independent trip. Go on a cruise, stay in a villa, or have an adventure! The world really is your oyster!

Check in with yourself

How do you feel? If you're not practically jumping up and down with excitement, something's not right. Be honest with yourself about what's going on and revisit some of the earlier chapters.

If you're feeling stuck on your plan? Here's an example:

I want to go to the South of France because I've been obsessed with the French culture for as long as I can remember! Going there will be a dream come true! I want to try as much French food as possible (yum!), stroll through colorful local markets, and visit several vineyards to taste the wine and learn about traditional wine-making methods. I want to see the lavender fields in Provence when they're in full bloom; I might even fly over them in a hot air balloon! So, I need to visit in early July – because that's when the lavender is out. I need at least 10 months to save, so I'll plan to go in July next year. I'll travel with my husband – maybe we can rekindle some romance in our relationship! I really like the idea of traveling just the two of us and staying in a little French villa in the countryside. But I definitely want an expert to plan our trip. I want to make sure we have the best possible time, plus I've no idea where to start!

CHAPTER 8:

Your Objection Action Plan

Now your dream bucket list trip is taking shape, it's time to dig deep and call out all the things that are **holding you back** from making it a reality. You can do this!

Nearly all the people I've helped take their dream vacation had to overcome some personal challenges. We're talking about you traveling to a place you've always dreamed of, but never thought you'd see for real – it's huge! So, it's natural for you to feel scared, apprehensive, doubtful that you can make this happen... But all the evidence suggests that you can – *if you really want to!*

The **top five** objections I've seen are:

1. **Time** – not enough vacation days.
2. **Money** – can't afford it; can't justify it.
3. **Others** – permission; what people will think.
4. **Fear** – of the unknown; of not accomplishing this dream.
5. **Shame/self-doubt** – don't deserve this; can't do this.

See? You're not alone! But you do have some work to do... The only way you can overcome your own challenges and objections is to identify them. Then decide how you'll deal with them, one at a time.

Take control of your life with the help of some self-reflection

How often do you ask yourself questions about your thoughts, feelings, and the way you act? Or wonder how you could have done something differently to achieve a better outcome? Self-reflection is a process you can use to get to know yourself and create more of the things in life that are important to you (like your bucket list trip!).

When you start to question what's causing you to behave or react in a certain way, it's easier to figure out what you can change to achieve the outcomes you want. Even simply realising that *something* is holding you back can make a big difference. If it's an actual problem, you can work towards finding a practical solution. If it's a negative thought pattern that's creating a block, can you be compassionate with yourself and just acknowledge it? The moment you become conscious of it, the thought will have less influence over you.

When you practice self-reflection, you move from the passenger seat into the driver's seat of your life! YOU get to be the one in control of your life and choices.

You can use self-reflection only when you're feeling stuck, or for best results, build it into your daily or weekly routine. But for now, it's time for some self-reflection to help make your bucket list trip a reality! Grab a pen and your **bucket list trip notebook**. When you put pen to paper it slows you down and gives your brain time to go deep *and* come up with creative solutions.

What's holding you back from making your bucket list trip a reality? Why can't you make it happen?

1. Write down **every** thought that springs to mind. Don't judge or try to come up with solutions just yet. When you think you've finished, give it another couple of minutes and see if you can think of anything else.

2. Take a quick break to reset – make yourself a drink!

3. Review your list; carefully consider each objection one at a time and ask yourself *does this thing really stop you from taking this trip?* If it's a resounding YES, then underline it. If it's a NO, keep going. (Not underlining something doesn't mean it's not relevant. By adding it to your list, you're now aware of it. You can recognise it when it comes up and remind yourself that it doesn't actually stop you.)

   Come back to each of your underlined objections and decide if it's a
4. mental, logistical, or financial challenge. Note M, L, or F.

DEALING WITH YOUR MENTAL CHALLENGES

You already know that mental challenges are **in your mind**. This means you've consciously or sub-consciously created the blocks you're now facing. It also means that you can uncreate them, but it takes effort.

Mental blocks are essentially limiting beliefs - you don't believe in yourself or in your ability to do something.

The great news is, you've just identified your mental blocks (relating to your dream trip in any case). You recognize that these things are holding you back, so now you can face them head on.

Consider each mental challenge you've underlined and answer these questions. (*Remember, writing gives you time to think, process, and be creative*):

- **Do you know where this mental block came from?** What caused it? Something in your past? Note down any potential cause as well as how it makes you feel.

- **How can you transform this limiting belief into an empowering belief?** What would it look like if you turned it on its head to your advantage?

For example, your limiting belief: *"I'm scared because I've never done anything like this before and I've no idea what to expect or if I'll even cope. I'd love to take this trip, but the idea terrifies me."*

Could become this empowering belief: *"I'm nervous about taking this trip, but I'm also really excited! I've never done anything like this before, but that's why I want to do it now. I want to do something new and exciting for myself whilst I have the chance! I'm not sure what to expect, but I can do lots of research before I go and make sure I'm well prepared. I know that I'll have an amazing time! I've been through so much in my life, it's not a dream vacation that's going to cause me problems! And I know I'll be well looked after because I'm traveling with Claire!"*

This stuff isn't easy. If it was and limiting beliefs didn't exist, we'd all be perfect human beings in a perfect world...

But you do have the power to overcome your mental blocks.

Be kind to yourself as you confront this knowledge and work to understand why you think and feel like this. Take as much time as you need. You might reflect on a particular issue for weeks or months before you clear the block and find peace. Life is all about the journey – not the destination.

DEALING WITH YOUR LOGISTICAL CHALLENGES

In your **bucket list trip notebook**, write down each logistical challenge you've underlined and the action/s you can take to overcome each objection. For example:

Logistical Challenge #1: *I had a recent health scare, and I don't even know if it's safe for me to get on a plane.*

Actions I can take: *Make an appointment with my doctor to discuss.*

Logistical Challenge #2: *Getting the time off work.*

Actions I can take: *Check the company policy on taking leave, then organize a meeting with my boss to discuss potential options.*

If you can't think of an action you can take – you've really no idea how to deal with this thing – try searching for ideas and inspiration online. These days you can find blogs and articles about literally everything!

DEALING WITH YOUR FINANCIAL CHALLENGES

You might discover that your finances are not as challenging as you thought (and if they are, you'll find a way). It's easy to spend money when it's there. You might find that you're buying all sorts of things that you don't even need. If you start putting this money in your savings fund instead, you'll be packing your suitcase in no time!

Let's figure out your budget and see what you're up against. Still working in your notebook, copy and complete the following:

A) **Approximate cost of my trip:** *$X*

B) **I'd like to take my trip around:** *Month, Year*

C) **Which gives me _____ months to save up.**

Divide the trip cost (A) by the number of months you have available to save up (C), to find out how much you need to save each month. Example: *$2,400 / 12 months =* ***$200 per month.***

Now work out your monthly household budget to see what's possible. Note down every expense you have, here's a list to get you started. If the expense is variable, do your best to estimate an average monthly spend.

- Mortgage/Rent
- Utilities (gas/electricity/water)
- Property tax
- Phone
- Internet
- Cable
- Insurance (car/home/health)
- Credit cards
- Loans
- Childcare
- Cleaner/window cleaning

- Pet supplies
- Health/Fitness/Sports
- Subscriptions (Netflix, Spotify, etc.)
- Gas, road tax, and parking
- Groceries
- Restaurants/fast-food/Take Out
- Entertainment
- Clothing
- Gifts
- Personal care (hair, nails, etc.)
- Any other non-essential spending

A) Total monthly expenses: $X

B) Total monthly income (paycheck, side hustle, other income sources): $X

Calculate your total monthly income 'B' less total monthly expenses 'A' = $X

Now you've calculated your disposable income – what you have left each month, decide how much you can realistically allocate to your BUCKET LIST FUND savings account. You might realise you already have the monthly amount you need to save for your trip. Sure, you might have normally spent that on little luxuries throughout the month. But you've decided to make saving for your dream vacation a priority instead!

**BUCKET LIST FUND savings account
monthly contribution:** $X

If you don't have enough left over to save the amount you need, keep going with the following steps:

1. **Review your budget** and see if there's anything you can cut back on or do without for a while.
2. **Check your subscriptions** – are you using them? Can you live without them for a few months and pay for your bucket list trip instead?
3. **How can you be thrifty?** Can you cut back on your budget for gifts, non-essential personal care, Take Out coffees and lunches, or another non-essential expense?

Now adjust your budget and see if you can do it!

If you're still struggling to come up with the monthly amount you need to save, think about how you can increase your income (chapter 6).

I know it feels hard, and that you're making sacrifices that will affect your day to day living over the next few months. It's your decision. But if you want my advice, I'll say once more for the record...

This trip will change your life in so many ways; you'll feel ever grateful to yourself that you made it happen!

Focus your mindset on the fact that **you're going to find the money** to make your dream come true. As soon as you **start thinking and feeling abundant**, the money energy will flow your way.

If you're serious about this, it's going to work.

There's no challenge you can't overcome to make your bucket list trip a reality. This is crunch time!

Believe you can do it.

Know you can do it.

Do it.

CHAPTER 9:

Set Yourself Up For Success!

You're ready! You've designed your dream trip, so you know exactly what's at stake and just how much you want this. You know **how** to approach any challenges standing in your way. So technically, you're all set. But, if you've got a long wait before your actual vacation, you're going to need some help to stay motivated and see it through...

Many people have dreams but never actually do anything about them. They procrastinate and then life gets in the way. Others are focused on their end goal – they really want to make it happen – but they don't have a process to achieve it. Hoping and praying won't get you anywhere unless you **take action, and for that you need a clear plan.**

Now it's time to pull everything together and set you up to succeed!

SETTING GOALS

Before you decide this chapter's either unnecessary or not for you, hear me out! This isn't about making your trip preparation rigid and dull. It's about maintaining that strong sense of excitement and **making your trip a reality!**

Your ultimate goal is of course taking the trip itself.

"I'm going to Costa Rica in April next year!"

But, if you've got a lot to do to make it happen between now and then, you need a tried and tested way to keep on track. That's where goals come in. The moment you start taking action towards achieving them, your trip will become more real, and you'll become more determined.

> When you achieve a goal – enjoy a sense of pride and feel your self-confidence skyrocket! This jolt of motivation will propel you towards checking off your next goal, and so on...

Mini goals (larger goals broken down into bite-sized goals) are the way to go! They feel more achievable *and* realistic – because they are! It's easy to visualize the very next step and focus on that. There's no need to get bogged down by your whole list or your end goal, which quite frankly might still feel very overwhelming!

How to set goals

You've already identified all the key actions you need to take to make your bucket list trip a reality. If you haven't got them all written down in one place, now's the time – grab your **bucket list trip notebook**.

Now consider each task/action. Is it clear cut? Or do you need to break it down? For example, having a meeting with your boss to agree a solution to get the time off work could be one goal. Or making the deposit payment on your trip – now that's a goal worthy of champagne!

Saving the full amount for your trip on the other hand is going to take time, so mini goals are perfect! Let's say you're already planning to save $1,500 over 10 months, $150 per month. Rather than set a goal of $1,500 in 10 months' time, set a goal of $450 in 3 months. Don't you think it feels more achievable? And if you manage to add a few extra dollars here and there, you could easily exceed your initial savings goal! In just three months, you'll feel like you're already well on your way to saving enough money for your trip *and* you'll feel motivated to keep going!

You decide what's going to work for you and set mini goals that feel realistic and achievable. You might end up with a long list, but it's not a problem since you'll be focusing on just one or two at one time.

Each goal should be specific and have a clearly defined timeline – the **action** you need to take and by **when**. Without a commitment, it's too easy to put things off and even give up. And don't forget to celebrate and reward yourself for every single win!

Check in on your progress against your goals at least weekly – set a reminder if you need to, but hopefully you'll have enough visual reminders around the place...!

VISUALIZATION

A great technique to use regularly is visualization. You can actually train your brain to make your bucket list trip a reality!

Try this quick test. Close your eyes and imagine biting into a juicy, delicious orange. Can you feel your mouth start to salivate? (Mine is just writing this!). There's no real orange, but your thoughts start a chain reaction, and your brain sends the same signals to your body, as if you're eating a real orange.

So, if you regularly close your eyes for a few moments and imagine yourself in your dream destination in as much detail as possible, your trip will become more real to your brain, making it easier for you to check off tasks and achieve goals.

Make a vision board!

Even if arts and crafts isn't your thing, making a vision board and looking at it every day, is sure to keep your eyes on the prize!

Find photos, images, quotes, or any other visuals that jump out and remind you WHY you want to make your bucket list trip a reality. Cut out a photo of yourself and add it to a spectacular image of your dream destination. It's only a matter of time before you'll be there for real!

Making a vision board is really simple and effective! Think about the kinds of activities you plan to do, the food you want to eat, the nature you want to see, and find these images. You can source millions of free images online without having to sign up:

- pixabay.com
- unsplash.com
- pexels.com

Don't forget to add a savings tracker – you know, like a thermometer you can color in as your BUCKET LIST FUND grows. Now *that's* going to feel satisfying!

Display your vision board in a prominent place – somewhere you'll see it every day. When you do, imagine standing in your dream destination and feel that renewed burst of excitement!

Don't fall into the trap of seeing your board but not *really* looking at it. Each time you see it, stop, and take a very deep breath – or three. It's a helpful way to remind yourself to take it all in – the more you visualize, the more real it becomes!

GOAL REMINDERS

Working towards mini goals, regularly visualizing yourself in your dream destination, and looking at your vision board will be great motivators. But when it comes to motivation, we can never have enough!

Goal reminders are another great way to stay motivated. I'm not talking about deadlines! Find something or several things related to your bucket list destination that will keep your dream alive:

- A physical object like a souvenir or something typical from the country you want to visit.
- Taste food and drink or try making recipes from your dream destination – you could even host a themed gathering or dinner party!
- Watch a movie that was filmed in the place you're longing to visit.

Leap at any opportunity to get excited about your trip all over again!

ACCOUNTABILITY

Recruit others to support and encourage you as you progress towards your ultimate goal of making your dream come true. Share your dream and your detailed plans with those you trust. People who will check in regularly, hold you accountable in a **positive way**, and help you get back on track if you lose confidence in yourself.

If you're taking this trip with a friend, you can become each other's accountability partner. This means you'll help and support each other to achieve your respective goals. If not, do you have a friend who has a different goal of their own? Can you share your plans and check in with each other regularly to help you both stay on track?

Join our Facebook Community!

If you're on Facebook, connect with others who are as determined as you to make their bucket list trip a reality. It's a great way to give and receive support, stay accountable, and share your progress with others. You'll find lots of tips and useful information to help you prepare for your trip and maintain momentum, and if you're struggling to overcome a particular challenge – ask the community for help. Best of all, enjoy being part of a supportive group who'll actively cheer you along. You may even meet people who are taking the same bucket list trip as you!

https://www.facebook.com/groups/bucketlisttraveltrips

For the latest information and inspiration about bucket list group trips you may want to join, this is the group for you:

https://www.facebook.com/groups/islandgirlbucketlisttrips

GETTING BACK ON THE HORSE

If life gets in the way, which it inevitably does sometimes, and you fall behind on your plan, don't beat yourself up. Instead, set aside some quiet time for self-reflection (chapter 8) and be honest with yourself.

Remember all the reasons WHY you decided to make this trip happen – nothing should stand in your way!

Review your trip notes and rekindle that 'can do' attitude! Then adjust your plan timelines if you need to and commit to achieving your next goal. No harm done.

If you start doubting yourself or asking questions about whether you really can make this trip happen, skim back through this book and find the inspiration and reassurance you need to keep going. Or find a supportive friend and talk it through. Sometimes, a little encouragement is all it takes to reset and refocus. You can do this!

MAKE YOUR BUCKET LIST TRIP A REALITY

You now have all the tools you need to make your dream come true. The only thing standing in your way is you. When you're nearing the end of your life, what would you like your final thoughts to include?

I really wish I'd taken that trip.

Or

I've had incredible experiences, seen amazing places, and truly lived my life to the full.

CHAPTER 10:

Travel Inspiration

Now you know you can make your bucket list trip a reality, you can go anywhere!

If you need some inspiration, take a look at my personal Top 20 Bucket Lists. Many of these destinations will be future bucket list group joining trips, so be sure to keep an eye on my website and Facebook groups or get in touch to register your interest!

My 'Trip' Bucket List (Top 20)

1. Tahiti, Bora Bora, Moorea, Tetiaroa
2. Antarctica– Polar Expedition
3. Peru – Macchu Picchu
4. African Safari
5. Greek Islands
6. Italy
7. Thailand
8. Galapagos Islands
9. Australia/New Zealand
10. Egypt/Holy Land
11. Maldives
12. Seychelles Islands
13. Patagonia – Argentina and Chile
14. Paris, France
15. Bali, Indonesia
16. Iceland
17. Trekking in the Himalaya
18. Climbing Mount Kilimanjaro
19. Petra, Jordan
20. Fiji and Cook Islands, South Pacific

My 'Experience' Bucket List (Top 20)

1. **Antarctica** – seeing the penguins!
2. **Botswana** – seeing elephants crossing the Chobe River.
3. **Tetiaroa, Tahiti** - remember that tropical paradise we talked about?
4. **Peru** – hiking the incredible Inca Trail at Machu Picchu.
5. **Iceland** - snorkeling between continents!
6. **Monaco** – seeing a Formula 1 race and staying on a Super Yacht!
7. **Thailand** – jet-skiing in the Andaman Islands.
8. **Uganda** – Gorilla trekking.
9. **Italy** – driving a Ferrari on the Monza racetrack.
10. **Cambodia** – visiting the stunning temple of Angkor Wat.
11. **Australia** – snorkeling or diving the Great Barrier Reef.
12. **Peru** – swimming with sea lions.
13. **Singapore** – dining at a Michelin star restaurant.
14. **Iceland** – seeing the Northern Lights.
15. **Greece** – island hopping!
16. **US** – visiting Grand Canyon and other National Parks.
17. **Borneo** – seeing orangutans.
18. **Zimbabwe** – taking a helicopter ride over Victoria Falls.
19. **Alaska** – cruising the spectacular coastlines.
20. **Croatia** – sailing in the azure blue Adriatic Sea.

Visit my website:

www.bucketlisttraveltrips.com

to see lots of great trips that you can take either independently or in a group - many led by me! Trips and ideas are constantly updated. Make sure to **complete the contact form** so we can connect! Also, **join our Facebook Groups** and be a part of our Bucket List Travel community.

www.facebook.com/groups/bucketlisttraveltrips
www.facebook.com/groups/islandgirlbucketlisttrips

Even more travel ideas!

- Challenge yourself to do something amazing like hiking the Camino trail in Spain, trekking to Everest Base Camp, hiking in Patagonia, or even climbing Mount Kilimanjaro! When you undertake these incredible mental and physical challenges, you'll discover a new sense of self and a feeling of accomplishment that will blow your mind!

- Go island-hopping in the Greek Islands to see the amazing beauty, and wildly varied geography and history between each of the islands.

- Choose Japan for a stimulating combination of ancient tradition to the super-futuristic modern! From towering Tokyo, to the Buddhist temples and stunning Mt Fuji. Stay in a traditional ryokan and really soak up local culture in onsen hot springs; learn about kimonos and Geisha culture in Kyoto. Participate in a traditional tea ceremony and sample the incredible varied Japanese cuisine.

- Stroll around Paris like a local! Wander along the banks of the Seine or take a river cruise and enjoy this romantic city from a different viewpoint. Meet Mona Lisa in The Louvre; head up the Eiffel Tower; take the Metro to Montmartre – the home of the famous Moulin Rouge and climb the white steps of the Sacré-Coeur. Soak up the history and architecture of the Notre-Dame and many other stunning churches, palaces, and museums. And don't forget to stop for a delicious espresso and pain au chocolat!

- If you're dreaming of Italy... Embrace your inner artist as you explore picturesque Italian villages, medieval towns, and sip on delicious wines at local wineries. Rent a scooter and zip along the country roads surrounded by rolling hills covered with vineyards and dotted with beautiful villas. Experience the history, art, architecture and museums. Wander down endless alleyways and find hidden gems - amazing restaurants with endless regional specialties sure to delight your inner foodie... You can even take some cooking classes with a local chef and perfect your fresh pasta-making technique!

- Visit Kenya to learn first-hand how the Maasai Warriors tend to their cattle and protect their tribe; how in Maasai culture, it's a woman's job to build the house using mud, sticks, grass, cow dung and cow urine; why the Maasai men jump so high when they dance and the significance of the beautiful red blankets and beaded necklaces that they wear.

- Go trekking in Northern Thailand where the most colorful and unchanged traditional communities can be found. Hike through forests and rural terrain to visit some of these diverse hill-tribe villages. Discover unique languages, clothing styles, and belief systems that differ significantly from those of neighboring tribes. Learn about bush food and medicinal plants and woodcarving and weaving, practiced the same way for centuries.

- Attend a local music or dance festival – maybe even learn a dance or two, or a how to play a new instrument? Attend a theatre performance – a West End musical in London, the ballet in Paris or an opera in Vienna... How about finding the love of your life at Europe's biggest singles festival which takes place every September in the small village of Lisdoonvarna on Ireland's Wild Atlantic Way?

Visit my website:

www.bucketlisttraveltrips.com

and discover lots of great trips that you can take either independently or in a group - many led by me! Trips and ideas are constantly updated. Make sure to **complete the contact form** so we can connect! Also, **join our Facebook Groups** and be a part of our Bucket List Travel community.

www.facebook.com/groups/bucketlisttraveltrips
www.facebook.com/groups/islandgirlbucketlisttrips

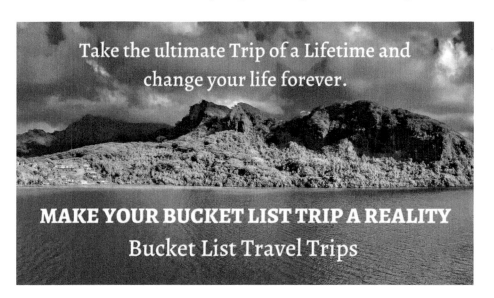

www.bucketlisttraveltrips.com

The Author

Claire Maguire Is a Travel Expert and self-confessed 'Travelaholic' (100 countries visited and counting, and all 7 continents!) who helps people to create and realize their Bucket List Dream trips. She loves to create priceless memories for her Travel Agency Clients and is now sharing her passion and knowledge with her new book, Make your Bucket List Trip a Reality! Affectionately known to clients, friends and industry colleagues as 'Upintheairclaire', she lives up to the moniker by traveling as often as possible. Her recent trips to the Monaco Formula 1 race, Antarctica and Tahiti fulfilled her own Bucket List but she is always adding more! Her other favorite destinations are South Africa, Thailand, Croatia, Greece, and Italy.

Printed in Great Britain
by Amazon

13010744R00047